NEW YORK REVIEW BOOKS

POETS

SZILÁRD BORBÉLY (1963–2014) was born in Fehérgyarmat in eastern Hungary and studied Hungarian philology and literature at the University of Debrecen, where he later taught. An authority on Hungarian literature of the late-Baroque period as well as a writer, Borbély was awarded several literary prizes, including the prestigious Palladium Prize in 2005. His first major critical success was his third book, *Hosszú nap el* (Long Day Away, 1993), praised by such writers as Péter Esterházy and Péter Nádas. His verse collections *Halotti pompa: Szekvenciák* (Final Matters: Sequences, 2004) and his novel, *Nincstelenek* (*The Dispossessed*, 2013), are considered among the most important Hungarian works of literature of the early millennium. His poems have appeared in English in *The American Reader*, *Asymptote*, and *Poetry*. *Berlin-Hamlet* is his first full collection to be published in English.

OTTILIE MULZET received the Best Translated Book Award in 2014 for her translation of László Krasznahorkai's *Seiobo There Below*. Other translations include Borbély's *The Dispossessed* and Gábor Schein's *Lazarus*.

Borbély

Berlin·Hamlet

TRANSLATED FROM THE HUNGARIAN
BY OTTILIE MULZET

NYRB/POETS

 NEW YORK REVIEW BOOKS *New York*

THIS IS A NEW YORK REVIEW BOOK
PUBLISHED BY THE NEW YORK REVIEW OF BOOKS
435 Hudson Street, New York, NY 10014
www.nyrb.com

The translator would like to acknowledge the kind support of the
Translators' House in Balatonfüred, Hungary, where this book was
partially translated.

Library of Congress Cataloging-in-Publication Data
Names: Borbély, Szilárd, 1964– author. | Mulzet, Ottilie, translator.
Title: Berlin-Hamlet / Szilard Jozsef Borbely ; translated by Ottilie Mulzet.
Description: New York : New York Review Books, 2016. | Series: New York
  Review Books poets | Originally published in Hungarian (Pecs : Jelenkor,
  2003). This is a reissue of Mulzet's English translation edition published
  by Agite/Fra in Prague, 2008, with some corrections made by the
  translator. | Includes bibliographical references.
Identifiers: LCCN 2016021277| ISBN 9781681370545 (paperback) | ISBN
  9781681370552 (ebook)
Subjects: LCSH: Borbély, Szilárd, 1964– —Translations into English. |
  Berlin (Germany)—Poetry. | BISAC: POETRY / Continental European. |
  POETRY / General.
Classification: LCC PH3213.B596 A2 2016 | DDC 894/.51114—dc23
LC record available at https://lccn.loc.gov/2016021277

ISBN 978-1-68137-054-5
Available as an electronic book; ISBN 978-1-68137-055-2

Cover and book design by Emily Singer

Printed in the United States of America on acid-free paper.
10 9 8 7 6 5 4 3 2 1

[For Ilona • For Mihály]

Contents

1. [Allegory I]   3

2. [Letter I]   4

3. [Epilogue I]   5

4. [Fragment I]   10

5. [Krumme Lanke]   11

6. [Letter II]   13

7. [Mühlendamm]   15

8. [Letter III]   16

9. [Fragment II]   17

10. [Allegory II]   18

11. [Schöneweide]   20

12. [Letter IV]   23

13. [Naturhistorisches Museum]   24

14. [Fragment III]   26

15. [Herrmann Strasse]   27

16. [Letter V]   28

17. [Heidelberger Platz]   29

18. [Fragment IV] 30

19. [Letter VI] 31

20. [Allegory III] 32

21. [Kurfürstendamm] 34

22. [Fragment V] 35

23. [Stephansdom] 36

24. [Letter] 38

25. [Tiergarten I] 39

26. [Fragment VI] 41

27. [Letter VIII] 44

28. [Invalidenstrasse] 45

29. [Allegory IV] 49

30. [Letter IX] 50

31. [Magdeburger Platz] 51

32. [Wannsee] 53

33. [Fragment VII] 55

34. [Letter X] 56

35. [Allegory V] 57

36. [Alexanderplatz]   59

37. [Allegory VI]   62

38. [Letter XI]   63

39. [Fragment VIII]   64

40. [Tiergarten II]   65

41. [Fragment IX]   74

42. [Letter XII]   76

43. [Allegory VII]   77

44. [Flughafen Schönefeld]   78

45. [Allegory VIII]   82

46. [Fragment X]   83

47. [Westend-Westkreuz]   84

48. [Letter XIII]   85

49. [Epilogue II]   86

Notes   89

Translator's Afterword   91

*Nothing ever passes
as irrevocably
as the morning.*

Berlin·Hamlet

1. [Allegory I]

The pierced heart, in which lovers
believe, recalls me to
my task. Always have I desired

to be led. My father's spirit instructed me
in ruthlessness. What he missed in life, he now
in death wished to supplant. I did not

find my upbringing to be a comfort.
The spirit of our age is for me excessively
libertine. My scorn is reserved for the weak.

2. [Letter I]

At last I have a picture of you as I
once saw you. Of course not as when I glimpsed you
for the first time, without your jacket, bareheaded,
your face unframed by a hat. But when
you disappeared before my eyes into the entrance of the
     hotel,

as I walked beside you, and nothing as of yet
connected me to you. Although I longed only
for the strongest tie to bind me to you. Tell me,
don't your relatives pursue you altogether too much? You
     wouldn't
have had time for me, even if I had come

to Berlin. But what am I saying? Is this how I want
to bring my self-reproaches to an end? And finally,
wasn't I right not to have come to Berlin? But
when shall I see you? In the summer? But why
precisely in the summer, if I shan't see you at Christmas?

3. *[Epilogue I]*

[i]

I annihilate the similes, before my time
was to come. The entanglements of speech, like
nooses hanging before the watering-hole,
where the feral come to drink. There are those
who writhe for days afterwards in the snares,
and their cries, like Christmas-tree ornaments
stored away between layers of cotton in the mothball-
  scented
cupboard, will be enervated, rent through
with fractures. They disintegrate
at a single touch. Somewhere else, the wild pear, the rose-
hips fallen amongst the dead leaves, the cranberry
and the rare Cornelian cherry.

•

[ii]

The recounting of the drawn-out
scream exacts renunciation.
After all, what of the upheaval
of the correspondences?—you ask.
The cry rolling through the forest
which, as it reaches the valley, is but
an obtuse murmuring. The echo of the news
come from afar shall be its own
tardy arrival. The prologue
followed by suffering.

•

[iii]

In the undergrowth of the freshly planted oaks
here and there stand mushrooms on slender deer-leg
        stems. And if
you take them home, forgetting them on the kitchen table,
in the afternoon silence they swarm with worms. And
        somewhere
the deer themselves emerge. From the farther shore
they watch, from behind the knoll. Between their antlers
they still balance, soon to let it drop,
the golden apple. At times
something rings out, and they glance
uneasily, with nostrils flared, towards
the garden of the Hesperides.

•

[iv]

Crashing through the undergrowth runs
a creature, half man, half goat
or horse. Only its screams can be heard.
Blood trickles down the foliage.
Cherry-red, brick-red, magenta-
scarlet, like the mineral hues
on an airy watercolor-painted sheaf. Between the
desiccated edges of the color-patches is
much air.

•

[v]

This jug behind the vitrine has
the form of a simile. Dolphins
swim in the spherical blue,
while the mouth of the man bound
to the mast, like his upper torso convulsing,
refers to the tautened struggle
of his scream. Yet his cries
are illusory, and the wellspring of deception,
which, like a breath held
back, has hardly since reached
that ear for which it was
intended. For he says that
in this likeness there shall not
be even one sound. Just as in pure
non-existence, of which I cannot know.

•

4. [Fragment I]

Yes, I could express it simply by saying
that our conversation left in me
a vacant space. Since then, every
day contains this space.

•

The necessity of formulation,
to say what has happened to me
every day since then. Since we stopped
meeting, recollection

•

has replaced our talks.
Since then, there has hardly been a day
which has not contained something,
and the reverse is also true. Recently I have begun

•

to interpret my silences.
And I feel there are days
which expand into breadth. Every
moment a growing depth, which

•

hides them in itself. Everything
is placed in something else,
which then takes possession. One word
possesses another. A word itself, however,

•

is an idea. What I called the void
is also a part of something. Perhaps of
our conversation which somehow still
continues to take place. I think.

5. [Krumme Lanke]

It happened in the last days of the Reich, sometime in the
   autumn.
The leaves were falling, and the air scraped across the
windshield. Only the vent-window of the front door was
open, we both were smoking. We wore long
woolen coats, loose trousers, and battered thin rubber-soled
shoes, as one must at such times. The fast was not obliga-
   tory, due to
the blockade there was hardly anything to eat. Everyone
   was waiting,
for someone, for something. Fear slowly grew stronger,
as did the instinct of self-preservation. With our meeting
   we were
taking an unjustified risk. Our superiors certainly
would have denied us permission. There was, however, no
   more
sense in taking orders. From the moment of liberation,
tradition formed our only mandate. We did not
speak of that, but it was perhaps why we met, here, below
   Berlin,
where the sight of two men strolling in conversation
would not seem conspicuous. Their collars turned up, hats
   pulled down
below their eyes in protection against the gusts of wind
   coming
from the lake. From the corners of their mouths, pressed
   hard together,
a half-smoked cigarette. Because strangers regularly came
   here,
on the weekends, to row, to sail, to stroll around the lake's
   edge. To the south

of Berlin, below the city, this was the spot, Wünsdorf or
    Teupitz.
I no longer remember precisely. Years ago, before the feast
of the exodus, while we were thinking of the future, we
    walked next to
Krumme Lanke in the western part of Berlin. Our
    conversation
was more of a remembering, a revocation of all
that had happened earlier. Like a film being played in
    reverse.
We watched the ducks; they were mute. The swans were
    threatening,
like death. There was one boat in the water, which
did not move. With every word the mist escaped from our
    mouths.
For a few seconds, tiny capricious figures were described in
    the air,
then they dissolved. Perhaps we could have deciphered
    these signs, if only
we had known how. They were weightless, like sin.

6. [Letter II]

My dear and honoured Fräulein, given the great likelihood
that you no longer remember who
I am, I will introduce myself once more:

my name in Hebrew is Amsel. I was that
person who greeted you for the first time one
evening in Prague. And that same hand that reached

across the table, that very hand now striking the keys, held
your hand, which confirmed a promise
to journey to Palestine with him next year.

I have only one confession to make:
I am a poor letter-writer. And if I hadn't a typewriter,
it would be even worse, for if my soul

grows weary, my fingertips can still toil
away at the keyboard. If no letter arrives,
I am never disappointed. All the same, as I wind a new

piece of paper into the typewriter, I am
filled with panic, for I realize I have made myself look far
    worse
than I actually am. If this is true, I deserve it,

for why am I writing on a typewriter to which I am
unaccustomed? And if after all of this you were to feel
that I am an unsuitable travelling companion,

as opposed to my epistolary partnership, and for the time
   being
this would be your sole concern, there should be no
   decisive prior
objections. So perhaps you might give me a try.

7. [Mühlendamm]

Afternoon had arrived at the house. Light fell upon the
    porcelain.
And from the radio an actor recited rhyming verse.—
Autumn is as all else in this land. Streets,
the river bank, telephone booths. What cannot be said
is why it is so. The recounting, the preparation,
even earlier hoped for, becomes
repetitious. I observe displacements, while my descriptions
are prepared in advance. So on the left a playground, then
a brewery. You sense it from afar. Then
influenza and the accustomed hovering of consciousness at
    such times
explains lateness. From the branches,
suspended like a veil, hangs the breeze, the twilight.
    Preparing this description
I read a memorial plaque in the lane. Here stood Millers'
    Row,
only the draymen came here. When the banks of the
water-ways were still connected, this is where
the millers lived. Along the causeways of the dams
    connecting the mills
they drove. If you come here, do not question strangers.
Since that time, the streets have been windy. In the
    tree-lined alley, twilight is a woven veil.

8. [Letter III]

When on the thirteenth of August I glimpsed her for the
    first time,
as she sat at the table, I nearly took her for a servant-girl.

I wasn't curious. As I sat down, I completely
forgot the matter. A strong-boned, empty face, openly

wearing its emptiness. Her neck uncovered. In a blouse
without buttons. Her costume looked homely in every
    respect.

But later on it emerged that it wasn't like that.
Such close proximity to her body

was somewhat estranging. A nose almost
broken. Fair, slightly rigid, characterless hair,

a strong chin. Then I looked at her for the first time more
    completely,
as I sat down. And when I was already seated, all

was resolved. As I gazed into her face,
I saw my fate, enfolded in a mute smile.

9. [Fragment II]

On the theatre of speech we are all
like stumbling amateur actors,
mimicking the heroes of old.

•

They read to us from books,
tell us what we have to say,
should we make our entrance. If all that comes

•

to mind is to don the masquerade,
which could be anyone's. Every word
futile, which does not sever

•

that thread woven by
the Fates, the reticent midwives
of thought. For reflection is

•

boundless, while in place of
resolve and deeds, words
are contemplated. I say that the Fates,

•

omniscient, have woven my own speech,
the theatre-stage upon which we meet,
while I declaim to you. I am the prince

•

of simulation, worshipper of the arts,
and of momentous deeds. Of beauty, ultimate and final.
For whom murder is the truest art.

10. [Allegory II]

[i]

Do you know those secret places in the park
where the early morning fog weaves spider-webs
after the chill of midnight. It raises the tenuous
filigree. Threads the pearls, then
joins them together. And the park fills
with light, while the mist collects into drops
on the crests of the leaves, and from the heights
of the branches you are observed by watchful eyes.

•

[ii]

The breeze directs the fog on the arching wooden bridges
above the canal. Amongst the trimmed hedges
the warbling of thrushes is your accompaniment. Wherever
you go, you find cut flowers on the table
in every season of the year. And we look
at each other in the overheated room.

•

11. [Schöneweide]

[i]

I know this is the most difficult thing. How to let it end,
as if nothing had happened. Suddenly
things change: doors are opened which
until then were shut. I did not wish to speak of this
to anyone. That is how I left, without saying goodbye,
without bidding anyone farewell. Just visited a few
acquaintances, as before. I dropped in for a chat,
to drink a beer, to sit and listen. Sometimes making
a comment. I adjusted the telephone only to receive calls.
Paid my bills several months in advance. And had to pay
something else. I topped up my account,
so that there would be money in it.
No telling what could happen. Whatever.

[ii]

I walked for the last time along those streets
where I walked one and a half years ago, before I moved
    here
to the tower blocks. Amongst the pock-marked concrete
    slabs,
where my mood was always foul.
If I looked out of my window, I saw the wall of the
    building across
from me, stained grey and black from the rainy streaks
of scum. I watched people in their kitchens, talking,
    washing dishes,
smoking or eating. And they watched me, as I held
them in my view. Sometimes they quarreled.
From behind the closed windows came the sound of their
    shouting. My
spirits fell. I watched their mornings:
as they rose, got dressed, prepared
for their day. In the evenings the blue radiating light of the
    television shone
into their rooms. I stood for a long time in the slowly
    dying light.

[iii]

Then one evening, I observed
the lit-up windows of Schöneweide's ruined buildings
from the S-Bahn. And sometimes I would get off
at the airport stop. I watched the lights in the pock-marked
    sky.
As the planes landed and took off. In the evenings
teenagers on the platform always begged
for cigarettes. A box went fast. I
smoked a lot then. I would buy a carton
of Magnums from the Chinese or Vietnamese vendors. And
always felt afraid, but not so much that I failed
to bargain with them. I came from abroad, and these
    adolescents
particularly dislike foreigners. There was one boy, perhaps
living in the same district as I. He always
asked me for one, we often met in the evenings. Then he
    would
only say: *Feuer*? He didn't ask, it was
practically a command. I readily lit up his cigarette. He was
a mangy, lost soul. I pitied him. And I thought of my
    relatives,
the ones whom I could never meet. Who
hovered for a while above the German-Polish lowlands, as
dust and ashes. Perhaps that is why I wanted to look,
    simply
to observe, for months on end, what the sky was like over
    Berlin.

12. [Letter IV]

Forgive me for not using the typewriter, but I feel
this letter to be very urgent, and the machine isn't
quick enough for me. It is a lovely day, warm outside, and
    the window
is open. It is always open anyway, but that hardly

pertains to my apology. Today I came into
the office only so that I could write to you. And after
I got your address, I was still unsure, was it the right one?
For there is nothing sadder than sending a letter

to an uncertain address. For that is no longer a letter,
but instead a sigh. Then I needed only to ascertain the
    right geographic
direction, as this is always essential for a Berlin
address. I myself would have placed you in the North,
    although

it is a poor district. My memory is bad, and
what my mind has devised, I immediately forget. Letter-
    writing
is a wearying task. Just keep a little diary
for me, this is a more modest request yet provides a greater
    bounty.

13. [Naturhistorisches Museum]

In the Natural History Museum, from ten until six,
the past is an open book. The domain of minerals and
    stones
is seemingly without motion. In a series of
rooms, animals stuffed and preserved
in compliance with the inferred order
of creation. Desiccated bodies, dehydrated plumes,

down, hides. Glass eyes, lifelike.
Movement slowed down to infinity, fixed
by dead creations. Although their legs
are in the air, heads are daintily averted.
If seen from the front, the half-profile is preferred.
Representatives of the great species, blind objects

in the darkness. But after closing time, life
doesn't stop. In the ancient oak casements of the vitrines,
tiny parasites continue their labour with
that indifferent monotonous background noise,
as the narrator of a nature film
speaks. Microscopic fungi,

various life-forms of simple constitution
battle for survival. Then the fine tension
of the dramatic tremulo penetrating the
mechanical voice: *And the viruses in the air.*
When, in the year sixteen hundred and seventy-nine,
after the last occurrence of the Black Death, a memorial

was erected to the devastation, new explanations
were sought. In addition to belief
in providence, there was faith in mathematics,
then statistics. When belief was thrust aside,
the mythology of freedom replaced the cult
of the dead. The result was the rapturous

veneration of life, then of course
wars, revolutions. But the watchword
of bliss displaced all else. In time
evolution became the modern metaphor
of death. And all the while humanity
still knew nothing of bacteria.

In front of the display of the great carnivores a quiet
child next to his mother steps back and takes
her hand. And points to one of the creatures: *it looks
like daddy*. And truly, one could arrange the material
according to the sequence of likenesses.
Through the associative and metaphorical correlations,

in a language that knows no history.
On the glass of the vitrines the bacteria flourish, but then
comes the great cleansing, *fine da capo*. A meteor
striking the earth, or a strain of virus now
dormant in the Amazon. Supposedly the beginning of life
was an infection that arrived on a meteorite.

14. [Fragment III]

Our collaboration speaks to the long term. Performance
is my required comportment. I do not wish to dissimulate.
My need is for those who will know how

all of this will end. How can he be king who
sets the crown upon his own head, not knowing his own
    father.
He grew up as a street urchin, his words tongue full of
    curses. Only

at times does he speak in formalities previously studied, or
he is prompted. More like a pantomime: guard, executioner,
whatever part is assigned. I am the one instead of him

who must unravel the role he will assume,
if the scenario is finished. Others prepare his notations,
while I recite a monologue in the wings, where

no one can hear what I am saying. But even now I am not
wholly free. As if an actor were performing in my stead,
I twist the words within myself like a dagger—my wish.

15. [Herrmann Strasse]

When I came to Berlin, I no longer
wanted to live. Why isn't there a way, I thought, if
someone doesn't want to live any more, simply to disappear.

Just like this: the decision is taken, the desire is strong.
And that would be enough. No need for poison,
blood, vomiting, depletion of the vegetative system.

Everything that comes with it: the sphincter muscles
slacken, and everything held together until now by the
    tangled
knot of consciousness flows apart. In a word,

expiration. How much do you have
to want it? Or do you have to believe in it? In Neuköln,
I met several homeless men who spoke English.

The snow lashed down upon us. It was more like sleet.
The worst of it is when your clothes are drenched and
    freeze
onto the body. They wanted money for mulled wine. In a
    frost

like this you couldn't deny them enough
for at least one cup. From time to time the lights
of the planes arriving or departing from Tempelhof

Airport glowed in the evening sky above
the length of Hermann Strasse. I too would have liked a
    bottle
of wine and a gyros from the Turkish stand.

16. [Letter V]

If I come to Berlin at Easter, would you have an hour to
  spare,
so that I could visit you? It could be at any time, for I won't
have any other business in Berlin, save our meeting. I hardly
have a proper suit in which to appear before you. But that is
  truly

incidental. One easily slides into temptation, however. I am
  only
travelling to Berlin to show myself to you, the one misled
by my letters, so you can see who I really am. This could
  not be achieved in writing,
because I set myself against it: in the light of reality

nothing remains hidden. Presence is irrefutable. If only I
  will have had
enough sleep when I meet you. If only my knees won't
  shake. What
a farcical and vague monologue this is. If I travel,
I will be staying in the Askanischer Hof hotel on König-
  grätzstrasse.

17. [Heidelberger Platz]

After a while I began to prefer the other sort of station
indicator, its emphasis different among the blaring
announcements. Signaling the closing of the doors,
urging me to flee, so as not to miss
the last chance of connection. Only at Heidelberger Platz,
I didn't have to hurry. There were never many people here.
　　And if
I arrived from Krumme Lanke, or the city centre, then
I transferred from the underground to the S-Bahn here.
The underground station could have been built in the time
of the Reich, I always kept that thought in mind. Its scale
　　was exaggerated,
the vaulted waiting-room monumental. The proportions
　　appeared strange,
and yet tasteful. I liked to come here,
but I had a superstitious fear of the place. I sensed
a murder had once taken place here. Once when I had
the time, I decided to take a look at the square as well. It
　　was an autumn day,
and sunny, such days are rare. I walked around the square,
but was disappointed. All I found was the deserted
intersection of an undistinguished provincial town. The
　　concrete columns
of the S-Bahn withdrew among the trees, which
hid it with discretion. A bit further on there was a pharmacy.
Ordinary people went about their business. They glanced
at me with dull, purposeless contempt. Through the colored
leaves on the tree, some still were green.

18. [Fragment IV]

After a long absence you no longer seek new friendships,
for recollection is stronger than forgiveness. You
no longer seek correlations, should you find amongst your
    papers
a letter undispatched. Indeed, who was that "Honorable Sir"
    or "Dear

•

H," who could that have been? And why only the majuscule?
Could it possibly correspond to anything? For at times you
    write
most cursorily, your manner hasty and facile, replete with
    terse allusions, that
"your playing to the seasons, to the sycophants may be
    likened."

•

The words divulge nothing: was it reverence
or scorn speaking through your pen? Perhaps you were
    merely hoping
you wouldn't have to quit the scene, as if that might be your
    refuge.
And since then, sheer indifference. The more recent stagings

•

court sensation, yet are commonplace. Prince or clown, it is
    all
the same to them. I watch the scenery instead. In the
    courtyard,
shadows with mottled sunlight. The hour grows late, it is
    time to dress.
Tonight's programme: theatre, tea-cakes, and ennui. With
    smiles all round for everyone.

19. [Letter VI]

I arrived in this city only to discover: I now can see
in the mirror that shade who steals after me. If I had
journeyed among mountains, I would not have felt more
unfettered. During the daytime, I wander through the city,

and when evening comes, I return to my hotel room.
The terrace is narrow and confined, but I take with me a
small table, and a taper, which was placed
before the bathroom mirror, presumably if the electricity

failed. I seek refuge from the clamor. I ready myself for
    work,
but find I cannot write. And when, as if the travails of the
    entire
day have assumed memory's garb, and they materialize
around me, demanding to be told to what

use that day was put, suddenly everything shrinks
away from me. Once again I go out into the street. I try
to reconcile the objects to myself, so that I may receive the
    gift
of their names. I wander amongst them until morning, ever
    more

blissful. And forlorn, for my own is not among them. But
it is not that which saddens me now, for everywhere is
hers. Our walk yesterday through the Grunewald and the
    park are closer
to me now than the telephone here in the Askanischer Hof.

20. [Allegory III]

He did not like to engage in the continuity of slow narra-
    tion,
and the imaginings of novelists, which for a time
he had no patience to follow. Lengthy tomes exasperated
    him.
Why can't they cleave to the essence? he asked himself.

•

And yet: the intricacy and circumstance of narrative still
    captivated.
A long, long delineation, which tells so much about
one single movement. Seated on the S-Bahn, just like
that person, closed book in hand, like a

•

citation now strange and indecipherable. A mild
and dormant vista is secluded in it, like a
gentlewoman of times gone by, departing into the light. And
like this sentence, our path is barred on the road

•

along which that figure disappeared. The man walked
    further along Holzmarkt-
strasse, towards Jannowitz-Brücke, slow and visibly
laden with care. Here was the place, commonly
the theatre of their morning walks. Here emerged the
    thought

•

when in a trusting state, that one's story could begin. And
    at other times,
that here it could end. To step quickly onto the
arriving train. And to travel on the S-Bahn, circling
around the city, transferring from one line to the next,

•

getting off at the Hauptbahnhof, because the sight of the
   arriving
and departing trains was comforting. And because one
   suspected
the possibility of narrative. That here something could
continue which had begun somewhere else, or that here
   •
it could end. Beneath the trees, where we three walked,
   the preoccupation
of professional cares. But there was no desire for
an answer or pacifying conclusion. And thought lingered
upon the citation, as upon that child who entered life
   stillborn.

21. [Kurfürstendamm]

At the time I had no answering machine, so
I couldn't call myself. Ludicrous, perhaps,
even morbid, how secure it made me feel to know
at any time I could hear my own voice. There is a voice,
    however
mechanical, which is mine. I have nothing else, if I think
hard about it, which is certain, just this distant voice
which comes from a machine. And the fact that at any time,
from anywhere, I can eavesdrop on it. There is a room,
    where
I live, and in it is a little black machine, which
speaks in the empty room. It makes clicking sounds. Now
spinning forward, now back. It switches on, then off.
It devours the room. But then I still had no
machine, and there was no one whom I could
have called. Who would have spoken to me, and I would not
have to feel ashamed for needing this voice. Just to hear
someone speaking to me. I concealed my faltering, whim-
    pering voice,
my mask-like face with its wayward mimicry.
Perhaps it was on the KuDamm that I saw it in a shop
    window, reflected
back for the first time. What I could say
to it. Since then I have a machine, sometimes I call myself.
I patiently wait until the end of the message, and after the
    long whistling sound
I leave these words: "I will outlive you, you pipsqueak!"

22. [Fragment V]

I would hover upon the empty dream of pure nothingness,
and I would observe the measure of the distance
from Denmark to England's misty isles. If every morning
at dawn I didn't have to fear the arrival

•

of my torment, renewed. To rise in the morning,
gnaw upon a piece of stale bread, and after coffee comes
    the acrid
recognition: this acquiescence must be sustained.
To learn anew the ways of speech, so that lies

•

shall be concealed. Everything was so different
in Wittenberg—here I would sigh deeply, as in a verse
of olden times. All is naught but a game. —Beware, there
    lies the poison!
Like an earwig, such a mere tiny insect. But

•

I embellish, I know. Such reverie and
paronomasia could prove injurious! they used to tell me
in the German universities. Prince, this is *subiectio*—
thus spake the doctors. The prescription, accordingly:
    silence.

23. [Stephansdom]

I wonder what it was like two hundred years ago in this
immense cathedral, when there was still
no amplification. The pealing of the bells
would descend from the heights somewhere above,

while the organ's reverberations emerged from the stones.
    And slowly
from below arose a voice: *Dominus
vobiscum!* only then to plunge deeper,
ever deeper, into the depths. Like this evening,

and the deacons' vestments, blood-red. In today's
Holy Mass, we shall pray for the eternal
salvation of our sister Maria Todt—he states,
uttering the name with evident circumspection. The
    Apostle

Jacob, the Festival of the Brethren, who was and
was not: our brethren. The strange euphony
of the Italian accent of the ministrant.
In the congregation are tourists, people passing through,

all in search of their souls. Bodies
embarked upon a journey. The priest's fragile hands
hovering in the distance. Today's reading from
the Gospel: the two sons of Zebedee. A parable

of time, and of affliction. And yet of
something else. This cathedral was newly rebuilt
after the war, as were nearly all churches
in this city. But of the demolished synagogues, not

even one. May we gain
eternal life? The priest asks in the voice
of the dead. Then he speaks of the chalice.
At the entrance to the cathedral, the usual jostling and
    haste.

24. [Letter]

There can be much at fault with Vienna, although again
     you speak
well of it. I could hardly imagine you so disconsolate
in Berlin, and I'm certain you weren't when you were
     there. As far as I'm concerned, I won't be travelling

to Vienna either, not even in May. I felt ghastly
there. I wouldn't stroll around the Parliament again for all
     the treasures in the world,
gawking aimlessly at the Kärntnerstrasse, Stephansplatz,
     or the Ring,

I wouldn't sit idly for hours in the Beethoven or Mozart
     cafes, let alone the
Ratskeller, and I wouldn't even ramble just one last time
     by myself
in the Schönbrunn gardens on a chilly yet nonetheless
     radiantly sunny morning.

I could go to Berlin too, regardless of the fact that it
     certainly would not be
as favorable as Dresden, and I am afraid to go to Berlin.
I am afraid of the sight of the city's outskirts as they come
     into view, I am afraid of the station platform

where I craned my neck to no avail, I am afraid of the
     entrance to the Anhalter Bahnhof,
where I had to face the line of oncoming automobiles, I am
     afraid
of the copper doorknobs, worn down and luminous, as I
     place my hands upon them.

25. [Tiergarten I]

The names of the streets, like the arid branches of the trees
in the park, which today is a labyrinth,
my path leads me across the Bendler Bridge,

Friedrich Wilhelm and Queen Louisa,
they too were here, but I have come too early,
chill circles dissolving into each other,

the Hofjägerallee is a disappointment,
amongst the foliage the maiden Ariadne,
then she disappears again behind a kiosk,

if I could only be Louis Ferdinand,
the prince of the narcissus and of the crocus,
Luise von Landau has invited me

to tea, on the banks of the Lützow, then
across the bridge, facing the gardens,
where friezes stand on the facades of the houses,

caryatids, Atlases, stair-carpets,
the cherubs and the Pomonas, the stained-glass windows,
the door-knockers, the battered threshold gods

all admit me, the veil of Ariadne
flutters here, the silent seeds planted
thirty years ago in this garden and the paths

covered with thicket and now there too
are the Lernean Hydra and the Nemean Lion
somewhere, near the Grosser Stern, while

the rising breeze from Europe's past
slowly propels, with the dreams of the Hesperides,
the laden vessels upstream

on the Landwehr-Canal, and the sailors'
hearts are filled with the anguish of times gone by,
as they moor at the bridge of Heracles.

26. [Fragment VI]

[i]

Travelling renders me wordless. If I even deign to speak,
I leave the words behind me, like
loose coins on the reception desk. How many places
are there in the world, and in none of them will I find
    anyone
who will tell me if the realm of the spirits
belongs to that of the dead, or to the labyrinth of voices. I
    regularly
write to you of the stations of my voyage. It is you who
truly are a guest everywhere; I am but your guide.
I am the hand which points to something. And yet.
While travelling I shall grow verbose; still my wariness

•

is ever sharpened. I hope to be misinterpreted,
if the unexpected fortuities do not meet
with my comprehension. Those who return
to their loved ones say "Travel makes one
solitary." No home is mine, thus
words have become the way-stations of my wanderings.
As long as the concealments of my speech beget
miscomprehension, I am not free. For the spirit lives among
my words, and they must annihilate
all accustomed things. What you have left behind

•

shall return in your dreams. You see, I am here now and
    you listen
as the water lashes against the side of the vessel; then
on the path by the embankment, the rustling of trees. I
    hear

the drumming of horses' hooves on byways unknown. I
    indulge in reverie.
I do not write to you of what I have met.
I can produce no account. I reflect
excessively, like the rhetoricians, seeking
for logic among my pronouncements. The philosophers'
    cognitions
are not my own, though I too am a sceptic.

I do not believe in poetry. I was never even
amorous, though that was expected as well. Nor should you
believe it! At times I confounded myself with my pursuers;
I am aware of their notations. And of all they write of me,
only this is true: that I exist. Otherwise it is but

•

mere delusion. Their denunciations are based on fallacy,
if they believe I am equal to their incoherent
stammerings. The detritus of their jottings is vexing to me.
Attempting to wrench open the riddles of my speech shall
    make poets
of my informers. "The prince hesitates," they say,

•

"in his speech he quotes maniacal poets." My *ars poetica*,
if such exists, is one of irritation: the dialogue of spirits
and wastrels. The enigma and obtuseness of their muddled
    conglomeration.
Such is my destiny. I could not even tell a lie
without them. "If we comprehend well what you are saying,

•

with every word, Your Grace formulates doubts anew,
the comprehension of which, consequently, we could never
even fathom. As soon as we understand, we become
the victims of misapprehension. He lays a snare with every
    sentence,
he wishes to see us dead. We fear

•

he is preparing for murder. Be vigilant of your person,
prince!" Sooner or later their attentions will render me mute.

27. [Letter VIII]

So may I come to visit? If so, please respond in time
to the following questions: what is your telephone number?
   Shall I dress
in black, or would it suffice simply to arrive in my summer
suit? I would much prefer that, as it would be more conve-
   nient, or more properly

said, the former is virtually impossible. Shall I bring flowers
for your mother? What kind? I am going to stay in the
   Askanischer Hof
again. It is difficult to say what paralyses me so in your
   presence.
Why would I prefer to struggle like a beast on the forest's
   earthen floor? There must

be a reason, mustn't there? It terrifies me, if you say "I
   don't understand
what this is all about, he writes often enough, but there's
   no rhyme or reason
to his letters, I don't know what they're saying, we haven't
   grown
closer, and there seems to be no hope of that, at least for
   now."

28. *[Invalidenstrasse]*

[i]

I must speak of my fear. Of the mornings
when I awoke drenched in sweat. After dreams
without memories. And I wanted nothing. Simply to
    disappear. Silence,
muteness. I didn't know why. Then
it came to me: What would happen, if—? What would
    happen if
there wouldn't be anything any more. Everything I'm
    doing now
I wouldn't have to finish. All of those things
which I don't know how to do. At once to reach
the end. I should like to reach the end. Let there be an end.
I began to desire this. If I would depart. Perhaps then.

[ii]

Months later, walking through the Tiergarten,
I thought back upon this. While, exactly as in the place
from which I had come, black crows covered the trees.
Which were the same grimy black. Bare
wretched skeletons. And the sky was the same level
chasmless false ceiling, below which stood
smoke-coloured clouds for days on end. In complete
   immobility.

[iii]

Berlin, the City of Gods, has found itself again. Frantically
it has prepared. The radio unceasingly announced
an avant-garde exhibit that had been opened in the
Hamburger Bahnhof. I had trouble finding it. No such
    station
exists. Then it turned out that for some time the building has
served only as a museum. I got off the S-Bahn
at the Lehrter Stadtbahnhof station. I observed
how the river was being diverted. The river-bed was being
drained out, and barricaded with enormous sheets of iron.
    Machines
toiled in its depths. Then after walking a few hundred meters
further on Invalidenstrasse, I saw the U-shaped building
on the other side. The site of the exhibit of the work
of avant-garde artists. No trains arrive here any more.
I though how good it would be if exhibits could be held
in airport terminals as well. Once in Zurich,
years ago, transferring to a Toronto-bound Swissair flight,
I lost my way in the monumental building. The sight
of the motionless people on the moving sidewalks was
    haunting.
The tension of impersonal smiles and courtesy, gratifying
nonetheless. I had arrived at a non-existent terminus.

[iv]

The Hamburger Bahnhof resembles the Anhalter Bahnhof.
In vain I searched for it one afternoon, after I had finished
my work in the City Library, and I set off to stroll
on the banks of the canal. Following the map's instructions
from memory, I kept to a southerly direction. I knew that
    soon I should
have to turn left. But I only found a square overgrown
with green grass, where a vaulted portico stood. Later on
I saw a photograph of the building itself, as it had once
    appeared. After that
I preferred to walk on to the Tiergarten. I wished to avoid
the new construction sites. The breeze carried the
    rumbling of
the machines from Potsdamer Platz. I tried to go even
    deeper into the park
so as not to hear. The architecture of the twenty-first
    century was being prepared
in this district of government buildings. I watched for a long
    time, above the crowns
of the trees in the twilight, as the forest of cranes completed
    their sluggish machinations.

29. *[Allegory IV]*

If you survive the time of your passing, and that age will
    come
which resembles you, and you should then look back
and all that I was comes to your mind,
do not believe that you were but yourself, and not I.
•
Like the evening after the performance, it will be difficult
to tell what occurred and what did not; but know
that which blurred the lines between who I was
and my existence was merely a game. For
•
my being, occupied by the speech of others,
as I was present in the emphases, shall
again be conjured forth upon the stage, empty and
yet with meaning replete. Like a
•
face after the play, radiantly smiling, albeit cold
as the hearts' ice. "My face shall live
as long as there are eyes, as long as there is breath,
and you shall live within them," I say; although it is
•
not you and not I, simply the memory of
a lyric. And what this sentence has endured,
only you and I shall know. And it will still be read
when there shall be neither the player nor the play.

30. [Letter IX]

I had a day of leave from work, and by Friday evening I was
   already
in Berlin. I went over to her office on Saturday morning. I
   sent in
a visiting card, giving the name of a certain Gotthard,
so as not to cause disturbance. Then I waited. I was happy

to be there. She came out, a little surprised, but not
excessively. She was very kind, we stood and talked for a
   while.
At noon I sat down with her for an hour in a pastry shop.
   After work
we wandered about the streets for two entire hours. That
   evening she was invited to a ball,

for business reasons, as she said, she could not stay away.
   On Sunday
morning we strolled for more than three hours, then sat
   down
in a café. In the afternoon, I left. In a locket, which I gave
   her
last November as a present, there is my likeness,

and she showed it to me. She would never marry anyone
   else, she said.
She would never throw away my letters. She would not
   ask for her photographs back.
She was willing to correspond with me, but wouldn't mind
   if she didn't have to any more.

31. [Magdeburger Platz]

There was a time when the market on Magdeburger Platz
    recalled
the golden age of antiquity. Let us not think that they
    referred to this place
as *Markthalle*. The variegated plenitude of the goods and
    the wares awaited the hand's

touch. In the course of bargaining, the words of profferment
    and acquisition exchanged owners.
Foreign phrases were mixed into their speech, evoking the
    enticement
of distant lands, like the faint memory of the scent

of exotic fruit. Every sound was thrust back heavily from
    the vaulted ceilings
of the inner hall, then falling down to the flagstones,
    subsided among the sawdust
and the remains of fried fish. The flagstones damp from the
    water of the fish-tanks and the

mop-bucket, slippery from the scraps of the carrots and
    lettuce. In their stalls
enclosed by wire lattice, each bearing its own number,
    ponderous
tradeswomen reigned. The priestesses of Ceres, herself up
    for sale,

were the market-women, procuresses of the fruits of tree
    and field, edible
fowl, fish and mammals. And are not their bodies,

swollen beneath their skirts, the true bounty-yielding soil?
    Did not some god

of the marketplace heap the wares into their laps: berries,
    scalloped
crabs, mushrooms, mountains of meat and cabbage, while
    all the while imperceptibly
coupling with their loins? They gave themselves to him
    sluggishly, however. The silent

customers stared fixedly like fish at the Naiad's thorny
    cliff, from which
at times something dropped, without anyone noticing. The
    ancient charwoman swept it up
away, and if someone called to her, she was known as
    Echo, for she was mute.

32. [Wannsee]

But what has become of Otmar Freyherr von Verschuer,
the learned scholar of maniacal intellect,
who prized scientific achievement above all else?
Regrettably, that was all he valued!

Who received heads freshly severed, preserved in spirit,
dispatched by the Reichspost from the East, for
he marveled at the contours of the tormented children's
    faces.
And he had an especial passion for twins.

His assistant always sent, from the fresh pile of corpses,
body parts excised with anatomical precision,
guileless eyes, for his master desired this.
His collection is a rarity even today!

What has ever become of Georg Leibbrandt, Erich Neu-
    mann, Wilhelm
Kritzinger, and what of Gerhard Klopfer the lawyer, Otto
    Hoffmann
the merchant, and Heinrich Müller, who disappeared
    without trace?
And what ever became of the other nine?

On the twentieth of January, in the year nineteen hundred
    and forty-two,
fifteen men conversed in one of the villas of Am Großen
    Wannsee,
in a fog of acrid cigarette smoke and strong cognac.
The pungent odor hardly resembled that of blood.

And suddenly the Erfurt firm of *Topf und Söhne* began
to receive many unexpected orders. And no one
even asked: where is the mad Prussian officer?
And where the blue eyes of Henriette Vogel?

33. [Fragment VII]

For the prince aspired to irony,
and that is why he got murder in return.
In the course of his travels, probing into the enigma

between the words, he stumbled upon the incomprehensible.
In his letters to his father, who had dispatched him
to Wittenberg, he had to render account.

Someone amongst his retinue of attendants was preparing
     reports
about him. And once he knew this, he would occasionally
     attempt
to imitate the style of these communiqués.

He envisaged how he might appear to the one who
scrutinized those thoughts never uttered
to anyone. And then he began to observe himself,

as his informer would. Essential to apprehend
the designs of those who wished to punish
him for his unspoken thoughts. He knew

he would only prevail, should he discover
what his enemies had not yet considered, what they would
presently decipher from his nervous and precipitous gestures.

34. [Letter X]

In the best of circumstances I should come to Berlin
as a man ground down by insomnia and headache. My first
order of business will be to creep into a hole somewhere,
    and cross-

examine myself. And I will only have the right to come to
    you,
to visit you again in the Immanuelkirchstrasse, if I am
    somehow able
to free myself from that hole.

Only then will you see me as I should be. Now,
however, whether in the Askanischer Hof, in Marienbad,
or in the Tiergarten, you rightfully look upon me as

an errant child, madman or suchlike.
An errant child to whom you are gracious
more than he deserves, although your kindness should be
    merited.

35. [Allegory V]

They are always present in the picture galleries, they
bring their chairs in with them. Light collapsible
stools, like hunters or fishermen,

and they sit down. Their gaze is as if fixed
on a faraway point. Though the galleries are large,
what they watch is not so distant. Their implements lie

a little farther off. The easels hired from the museum,
with a small cabinet for all the necessary items.
On the tight-stretched primed canvas, you can see, if

you step closer, the outlines of the picture sketched in
    chalk.
Squinting, the tones and the masses of the bodies are more
    easily
distinguished. The vision of the celebratory throng is
    terrifying. The blessing

hardly blunts the disaster to come. These words are known
to the one who paints this scene anew. Seven times in one
    life,
as the years run their course, this picture will be copied.
    They stand

beneath the tent. One of them, who no longer exists,
    already wears
funereal robes. What is not yet real evokes the prohibition
of the graven image, he said, as we strolled on the banks of
    the Wannsee

after our engagement. We could have watched as the ships sailed and docked on the Landwehrkanal by the bridge of Heracles. The rings tight around our fingers. And yet still too young.

36. [Alexanderplatz]

On Alexanderplatz, by the entrance to the U-Bahn,
trampled cardboard. The square is being
rebuilt. Everything here is disciplined. On the ground
a paper box with a few coins inside. A Belorussian
opera singer's greatest hits. Beneath the arches of the
    S-Bahn
white steam in the lamplight. It drifts up from
the Weisswurst stand. Sitting at the bottom of the steps,

with their dogs, are teenagers begging
and smoking grass. The back of one hand tiredly drops
to the pavement. Between the fingers, at the end of the
    joint, the tiny bit
of ash trembles. Guest workers in grubby clothes
return home from the construction sites
in the centre. During the day I eat with them
at the makeshift kiosks. In the morning, frost-bitten grass

on the cold charcoal clumps of earth. The workers mainly
Slavs and Romanians, but there are Spaniards
and Italians among them too. The collectivity of people
    living
far from their families, in the depths of the winter night,
on the heated station platform. In the corner
an overcoat, a leg protruding, and people
stepping on it. From between the creases of fabric gapes

a face, like the countenance of Europe scorned. It spits
into the distance, but does not speak. It reflects,
like thought itself. Above, the floodlit city
looks to a new epoch. The escalator

rises into the heights, and creates correspondences,
like a metaphor degraded in the course of time
into a simile. The mind listens. Behind it, the train

pulls out. Ringing memories arise. The doors slide
shut. Attention, the train is departing, says the guard,
      presses a button, and
crosses to the other side. On the surface, a new
epic is being built. Because of the construction, the corridors
to the exit constantly shift. This is a veritable
labyrinth. Ariadne, my dear, I tell you

the exit is not far. The winter sky
clasps its fingers against the square, where in the
milky fog, opal from the lamplight, the vendors
prepare for Christmas. Light falls
on the cobblestones like battered straw. The man in a
      frayed
tuxedo and foam-white scarf, sings of snow-covered
Mother Russia. And before the path leads up

to the surface, edgy Vietnamese cigarette-sellers
seek out your gaze. From the obscurity here and there
one or two bends forward. The goods,
not his own, are in advertising-covered plastic
shopping bags. For a few seconds,
between interlocking pairs of eyes, the signal of
hatred and fear in the winter evening, from the square

emanates the jarring strains of *Stille Nacht*,
the melody familiar from being put on hold
at the telephone exchange. And as if the heart for now
and forever would stop, and something else, perhaps the
      land itself

would throb, and not cessation, and the degraded
foreign race would become conscience itself,
and the heart, the voice. At such times

the sky is low. The city itself is like the winter sky,
hanging in space, in its windows blaze
the stars. In the shop-fronts and vitrines
shame is on fire. The tired darkness, like
the hearts of those executed
at dawn, stands still. A raven flies across
the cold emptiness. Above the city rises the winter sky.

37. [Allegory VI]

Rain endures the longest,
and the thought
which will follow,
if it reaches an end.

Now only the tapping
on the eaves and streaks of water
on the pavement. The afternoon light
a thin layer of film

on the tree leaves, which
tinges them. The hues trickle like
watercolors, run together, they
smudge, follow the veins' path.

Just as thought
finds words, the afternoon
falls, like a curtain,
after sleep the button

of the pillow leaving an imprint
on the body's design,
as it presses into the skin.
Then come impressions,

like birds, as they slowly
oscillate, growing indistinct on the border
between the eye and the heavens.
For rain endures the longest.

38. *[Letter XI]*

Just now, however, in Marienbad I saw the trusting gaze
of a woman, and I could not remain aloof. Much has been
    torn open
that I would have preserved whole. Past this fissure, I
    know well,

there will remain sufficient misfortune. More than is
    needed for one
human life. These tribulations are not however the fruit
of defiance, but rather an inherent burden. I have no right
    to protect

myself against it, even less so because all that is happening,
if it were not, I would still cause to occur, just to allow
that gaze to be mine again. Until now I didn't even

know her: as she came towards me in the grand salon, to
receive the betrothal kiss, a chill went down my spine.
    Directly
once the war is over, we will be married. And I shall move
    to Berlin.

39. [Fragment VIII]

I can no longer bear the aggressiveness of poetry,
and I do not wish my deeds to be investigated.

I would like to be an opened knife: the inscrutable.
A razor-wielding murderer. With a tongue oozing flattery,
    who drips

poison into your ear. Who makes you mute, so you cannot
scream. As the guards turn into the corridor,

I count five steps. Now is the time to cry out. Before
they throw themselves on me. Then in the stillness, there
    are no sounds.

40. [Tiergarten II]

[i]

There was a day when my eyes grew weary. All morning,
I watched TV. Then I went to the movies. And I can only
recall that the film just wouldn't end. Then
nervously I got up, try to grope my way towards the aisle.
   Treading
on the feet of some people. Still saying
excuse me, as I come out onto the street. In the meantime
I watched the movement of the light coming from the
   projector,
the sudden alternation of colors and shadows
in it. This is how I spent the day. I was already bored stiff
   by the first one,
The Tempest. There was too much. Too much of every-
   thing in it.

[ii]

Why am I so intrigued by the disappearance of the body?
—he asked, as he came out of the *Kino* and looked up
at the sky, which now, as it already had for days, dully
and joylessly cast its grey towards the
restless, precipitous city. A sentence like that belongs in a
crime novel. It would incite the narrative of the maniacal
    assassin
or the still unsuspecting victim. He came out of the café
late in the evening, stopped in the doorway, took a deep
    breath,
turned up the collar of his coat, and looked around. He
    hurried
to the nearest S-Bahn station, and just in time
ran up the stairs. He forced his way into the carriage, the
    scent of a woman's perfume
struck him in the face. Calmly he looked back
at the platform slowly disappearing into the distance, at
    the man
running alongside it in an impeccably tailored trench coat,
    his face
ashen-grey. Apparently desirous of revenge, which is why
    he dispatched
the train. Only four stations to the Tiergarten,
must hold out till then. And then…? Then so many things
    could
happen. —This evening I will read the sequel.

[iii]

Lately I had been reading a lot of crime thrillers, and
    sentences
would form in my head which could have come
from a detective novel. He got off at the Tiergarten, after
    the movies
it was good to walk here. The park, its paths laid out on a
    radial plan,
the scent of decaying leaves, all made this place familiar.
On the long straight path, he started off towards the
    central point,
towards the angel at the top of the column. He thought
    about how
he didn't know what bonds tie memories
to the one who remembers. Perhaps just the sentences,
or simply a rough draft: the exact notation
of time and place. The rest are broken fragments fading
    into indistinction,
mingling with the over-sweet scent of the rotting leaves,
with the smell of the dogs belonging to teenagers
begging by the staircase of the Friedrichstrasse station.
    Then the
anxiety at the sight of the skinheads, still children,
their eyes innocent. How many generations of fear
gaze out from your eyes? Why are you so tired?
Was it all so ugly? Are you happy now? Would you
have believed it? —he asks himself, muttering. No problem,
    though,
no one here will understand. The many pairs of eyes, like
    from gilded wooden panels,

look down on me from the soot-filled heavens, from the
    burnished gold
of the evening sky, now I speak to them: I liked
the U2 video, when Bono sits atop the column, and you
    can see,
up close, the statue's pathetic face. I stand beneath it
and I cry out: "Angel, o winged angel, angel resounding
and white! Angel, o great winged angel!"

[iv]

Of course, it didn't happen like that. But on that afternoon,
at the beginning of November, I really did go to the
    Tiergarten
for a stroll, after I walked out of Greenaway's *Pillow Book*.
I really don't know why I didn't like it,
why it irritated me so. I watched the rooks, as they
swarmed the crowns of the trees. Some of them alighted
    on the ground, scavenging
among the dead fallen leaves. I met a few solitary
joggers, pursuers not of asceticism but of
pleasure. When the body is swept across the weariness of
    exertion, and
the hormones generated by the brain render the bounds of
    the self indistinct.
That is why I used to go running. But to stroll is in itself
    an art. It is easy,
like the blue parallel lines arising from the bowl of a
    pipe.—

[v]

That picture came into my head, I don't know why, when
in the doorway of a house in the Moabit district I brushed
    against
a monumental African prostitute, smoking a cigarette.
I was so astonished to see this colossal body for sale,
by no means a usual occurrence in this place,
that I forgot to ask: how much and what?
Just to know the price. I declined the offer, and quickly
crossed the gate connecting the two streets. The head,
its hair shorn like a boy's, resembled the angel from the
    U2 video. Her yellow-black
skin was nearly luminous. The lights sparkled on it. Her
    breasts
bulged out of the tight leather jacket she wore. Her
    powerful
thighs were hardly covered by the tiny, gaudy red
shorts. Her laced high-heel boots, nearly as black as her
    skin, reflected
the lights penetrating from the street. This dark body made
me think of a golden-hued statue. Yellow fog,
enshrouding the streets in its neon phosphorescence,
    billowed
between the trees. At times like this in childhood
I eagerly awaited the Christmas holidays. I imagined what
would happen if an angel were to appear before me. If with
    honeyed
harps, in pink-tinted light, the heavens would be revealed,
like in the Opera House. And I would laugh, and I would
    cry, and I would think

it was a dream. Instead of this, Christmas evenings were
    colorless,
the grip of anxiety never allayed. That face which I wear is
the imprint of this. It is calculated, like the cover of a book.
I head off to the Brandenburg Gate, wishing to avoid
the new construction sites. I look at the sky, and I muse
upon the empty dream of pure nothingness. What can it
    mean?

[vi]

How beautiful are the sunsets! How beautiful, under the
    vault of the heavens,
is the shelter of the earth. It is Friday, Friday afternoon, and
in a moment twilight will come. The city enfolds itself in
    mist, gathering
its memories onto itself. He watched, for at times like this,
    the people
moved uneasily through the streets. Perhaps they were
    seeking
their relatives, or the houses or squares where they had
    lived. From the level
of the second floor, where the S-Bahn tracks are, from the
    lit-up
windows, faces luminous and weary listlessly observe. At
    times, the lights
briefly go out. And sometimes the train stands still
on the open tracks. The day slowly ends. People returning
    home from work
buy the evening papers. And as in the mornings, waiting for
    the train,
they leaf quickly through them, and then cram them into
    the nearest bin.
He didn't understand this custom. He waited a while, for
    everyone to board
the train, and when it had left, took one out.
He read the evening programme. Then sat for a while yet
on the platform bench. He put on his baseball cap. Lit up

a match. Watched as it burned. Then a second one. With that he lit up a cigarette. He was about to turn 33 years old.

41. [Fragment IX]

Then we spoke of what bound us together.
It was already late when we sat down, after our meeting,
purely accidental. You having just arrived, whereas I
had to hurry off. I was startled, I wasn't expecting

•

this encounter. If I had seen a ghost, perhaps,
I would have been more surprised. It was already evening.
This happened in a shopping centre, where the crowds
    always
throng at this time of day. There are those who run in

•

simply to buy one item. Or simply to stroll, to take
    pleasure in the lights, the warmth,
or the teeming crowds. I had a meeting with a certain
security guard. A distant relative. Some murky affair,
which I no longer remember. People showing up for that
    evening's screening

•

arrive, precisely as the others leave. The rooms are
    ventilated
after their departure. The cool of the air-conditioning
    strikes my face,
a soft draught of air. Crowds swarming around the Chinese
    restaurant. Different scents
and tastes. There are those who like it. We spoke of such
    things. I endeavored

•

to knit the words together, so there would be no space
    between them,
no space to ask. Then we spoke of the weather. And I
    watched the security guards,

to see if my acquaintance was among them. I didn't know
what to say. I observed your shadow on the plate-glass
    windows of the shops

•

moving slowly with the contours of my own.
They did not merge together, and yet were not truly two
    entities,
just one. But I realized this only later,
and even then I did not attribute any significance to this
    phenomenon.

42. [Letter XII]

If I am not to travel to Berlin, my silence will not be
the cause. The true motive for my reticence is that exactly
four weeks ago, at five o'clock in the morning, I experienced
   a hemorrhage

of the lungs. For ten minutes or longer, the blood gurgled
out of my throat. I thought it would never end. The next day
I went to the doctor, who examined me. Then there
   followed

more examinations, X-rays, and a referral to a
specialist. The fact of the matter is that both of the lungs
   are already
afflicted. I'm not surprised that this illness suddenly

came upon me, and not even by the blood. For years now,
I've enticed it with insomnia and headaches. But that it
   should be
tuberculosis. Naturally, I'm surprised that it would

appear just now at the age of thirty-four, unexpectedly,
at midnight. Now I shall at least go to the country. I will
   depart
by next week and travel to Zürau, postal address Flöhau.

43. [Allegory VII]

The "heart which is free of all base thoughts,"
already having surpassed "the borders of beyond,"
and gazing back upon language, upon that costume
which was its body, the tapestry of speech,

•

which, as now it seems, has already departed,
without bidding farewell, and without looking back,
in its tread the voice of all that is irrevocable,
perhaps the misapprehension of things uttered,

•

or perhaps, on the contrary, the certitude
of silence, that strength which destroys,
and that *something* which is withheld,
until now unperceived and unthought,

•

like everything which is infinity's antipode,
the disavowal, that is, of time and of space,
at once the boundary and the unbounded,
which exists in this very word,

•

but not even here, for there is no looking back, for
there is no *backwards* and there is no *was*, and not even
memory to disturb his attention;
no telling what will occupy it now.

44. [Flughafen Schönefeld]

The edge of the city, once the realm
of foreigners, breaks apart like the
disintegrating margin of old pasteboard;
the breeze skims over and peruses it. Like
the impress of leaden type long ago
melted down, here the candelabra
watch over, on the iron vaulting of
the S-Bahn stations, the names of streets
and squares, which are legible once
twilight falls. Even before

I came here, I had a liking for
the name Steglitz. He was
a photographer, or something like it,
I'm not sure. Exchanging the silvered
copper-sulphate plates in his Rollex
camera, he applied a light-sensitive
emulsion, prepared by himself,
onto a glass negative, and in the
rooms thickly padded with darkness

called forth anew the city's streets, its squares,
its passers-by strolling and reading. From the
long exposure times, from the moonlight's
delicate filigree, he wove pale images, which
he tinted antique brown in a bath
of his own invention. And like cooled
lumps of ore, the eyes rolled all around
his pictures. Every evening, spectators
at the exhibition set off on a journey towards
the long-extinct streets, bars, air-raid shelters,

psychiatric clinics and insane asylums
of the Dahlem, Grunewald and Moabit
districts. The expanding city centre melted
them into itself; before the click of
the shutter mechanism, their consciousness
dissolved. And by the time the silver
of their blood trickled down
the glass negatives in their submerged
spiderweb-veined fissures, where

the police-boxes keep vigil in the U-Bahn
stations, German shepherds
with armed patrols began to sniff at
the breeze suddenly arising from the
tunnels. The arriving train pushes
the air before it, the dangling tongues
of the dogs behind the muzzles' cage, a tapering
thread of drool trickles onto the
cement. Farther on, teenagers
flee from their parents'
destiny, while bank-machine receipts

and clandestine underground cellars
are filled with the darkness of their lungs, and
the traces of vomit around the
refreshment vans. On either side of the puddle-lit streets
there are pubs and brothels,
Ausländers and on lascivious staircases
North African women await,
in the fissures of their dark skin
crimson flesh at times glitters,

congealed blood in the crevices of their lips.
The homeless tug at the buttons of the cigarette
machine, the contraceptive dispensers in the toilets, as
saliva drips down the pleading faces of
the insane, like a gramophone endlessly
repeating the memories of a
consciousness now lost. From time to time, someone
travels out here from the city center to research their
muddled narratives, averting as of yet
that disintegration which the houses,
the deserted allotments, the roofs,

and, rumbling by the first-floor
windows, the express train
all drag behind themselves in the evening,
like the anarchists' slogan remaining
on the firewall from the time of
revolution: SEI EIN REALIST!
ERFORDERE DAS UNMÖGLICHE! From the
bodies of the sleeping, the wavering vapors
slowly arise, the scalding miasma
of amorous couples, like
airplanes, machines which know no depth,

only surface, as languorously they ascend
onto the heavens of the evening. Their tiny lights
glitter in the coal-sludge darkness, which
sifts up from the industrial plants and
clings to the photographer's plate, like the moon's
silver, like amalgamate. The glittering mica
scratches the glass, sometimes a sharp
needle, sometimes a forgotten molecule,
the neon light above the enormous

buildings: FLUGHAFEN SCHÖNEFELD,
the last stop on the S-Bahn. Below the
runway lights, above the railway signals.
The machines, like the evening swaddled
in tattered oily rags, float across
the sky until tomorrow, when
they shall again reach earth. The passengers
inside are motionless, when from the recesses
they are discharged one after another into the night.

45. [Allegory VIII]

I perceived that the circle of my pursuers was closing
    around me.
I no longer returned to my favorite restaurants.
I changed my habits, evaded my former
trajectories. I burned my notes, and memorized
everything. I hurried, my steps urgent, along the system
of corridors and staircases connecting the underground to
    the S-Bahn
on Alexanderplatz. The long years of my childhood,
the stubbornly returning mood of its dream, repeated itself
in these days. But it all began late one evening
in a German city. After darkness fell, following a brief
troubled sleep, I awoke with a start. I met with someone
in an apartment, then had to flee through the empty
    streets.
In a violent wind we slipped across a small stone bridge,
in the frame of a doorway made ourselves flat. I do not
    recall
those who were with me. Only a few whispered words
could I hear, in a tongue unknown
to me. For years I felt, while I dreamt
this story over and over, that I would recognize
the city, should I ever come across it.
The ending of the tale was obscure. I was murdered, I don't
    know why.
I lay upon the cobblestones in a corner of the main square.
    The blood
ran from my head. The last picture my opened eyes
could still preserve: the clock-tower. High above my head
it struck pitiless into the glimmering blue of the glimmering
    dawn sky.

46. [Fragment X]

I have read through volumes, the graveyards
of their dead letters. I have walked
upon their weed-strewn paths, and met with no one.

Before me crept a snake, and this
he said: "You see, this garden is dead, like
your soul, parched with doubt.

For doubt has struggled with desire, desire
to relate what you only dimly perceive.
When you attain fulfillment, your desire hardly

abates. You merely jerk spasmodically. As long as
others still desire, you remain your organs' slave.
There is no face which you could discern

in this moment. You are blind, your eyes
seek a visage struck with horror.
That face which has begotten: that of the spirit."

47. [Westend-Westkreuz]

It is late autumn, the leaves are rustling, and as I walk
    through the Tiergarten,
I realized I had forgotten. That it was like this. They say
    this is the time to sleep.
To take vitamins, go to the sauna, and not watch televi-
    sion. Or only before
bedtime. To listen to music often, because it opens the ear.
    To travel
cautiously, so you may find your way back. That your
    heart may ache, as when asleep
on the S-Bahn your head nods to one side. This recurs in a
    rhythmical pattern, and
outside is the darkness. The lights disappear, as you pass
    Westkreuz, as
the train heads to the East. There are always one or two
    children playing amongst the commuters
at this hour, even in winter, even at the airport. Everyone,
    though, is at work:
reading, telephoning, tapping away on their laptops. Tired,
    sophisticated faces
for the most part. Impeccably knotted ties, pressed shirts,
    deodorant,
Swiss watches, signet rings. Order is created through pure
chance. Birth gives rise to chaos. No one says so, for death
is easier to regulate. To sit in a snug tavern, look at the
    hoarfrost-covered trees,
the snow, the lights, the city's dead empty squares. Where
    you are only passing through.

48. [Letter XIII]

My audacious undertaking was as follows: to
spend a few days in Berlin. Otherwise, here
in Steglitz, life is tranquil. I don't visit the
central part of the city, of course. My own Potsdamer

Platz is the square before the Steglitzer Rathaus. Palestine,
moreover, would be completely out of my grasp, and
consequently, taking the Berlin possibilities into
    consideration,
not even urgent. Of course Berlin too is very nearly
    unreachable

and it could well turn out that the Palestine voyage will
    shrivel
into an excursion to Prague. Let the matter rest there,
lest at the very end, I shall only be able to take the lift
up to my room in one of the lodging-houses on the
    Altstädter Ring.

49. [Epilogue II]

[i]

For the dead are expected to know the path
above the precipice of the everyday. When
they leave the lands of despair, and depart
towards a kingdom far away and unknown,
which is like music. Swelling, a solitary
expectation everywhere present. This music
does not break through the walls. It taps gently.
It steals across the crevices. Silently it creeps,
and cracks open the nut hidden deep within the coffer.
It sets in motion the glass marble believed lost,
it plays with it. Suddenly, the cut crystal glasses
begin to crack in the china cabinet. And the chord
    bursts apart.

•

[ii]

God's being is an open box, filled
with the dead. Thrown upon each other
they lie, and look far away
into the distance. They do not close their eyes, even
for a moment. God cowers and trembles
in a remote corner. Eyelashes convulsively
knotted together. In a thin
whimpering voice he cries.

•

[iii]

God's being is an open box, filled
with toys. Sometimes children sit around him,
they rummage through the box. Every toy is an
enigma. God sits among them, and
watches. He too is a child, who searches
through the toys. When he finds something,
he is happy. He turns it over a bit
in his hands. Then throws it back.

•

Notes

vi   The epigraph of the volume is taken from Walter Benjamin's essay "Weimar": "Nichts kann so unweiderbringlich wie ein Morgen dahin sein." (Walter Benjamin, *Gesammelte Schriften*, Fischer Verlag, IV/1, p. 353.)

1   In 1936 in Berlin, *Hamlet* was performed with Hans Höfgen in the title role.

4   For the cycle of poems entitled "Letter," I have used excerpts from Franz Kafka's letters as published in the Hungarian version edited by Miklós Győrffy and largely translated by László Antal (Franz Kafka, *Naplók, levelek*, Budapest, Európa Kiadó, 1981). I have also used as a source: Elias Canetti, *Der andere Prozess: Briefe an Felice*, München-Wien, Carl Hanser Verlag, 1976.

39   The poems entitled "Tiergarten I" and "Magdeburger
and 51 Platz" are partially based on the following texts of Walter Benjamin: *A Berlin Childhood at the Turn of the Century*, *Tiergarten*, and *The Market Hall on Magdeburger Platz* (English in: *Reflections: Essays, Aphorisms, Autobiographical Writings*, ed. Peter Demetz: New York: Schocken, 1986; Hungarian translations in: *Kommentár és prófécia*, Budapest, 1969, pp. 29-32 and 43-44.)

49   The poem entitled "Allegory IV" makes use of Shakespeare's Sonnet no. XXXII. Originally it appeared in Hungarian under the title *XXXII. szonett*, with a dedication to Gábor Czeizel and Szilárd Várnai.

53   The poem "Wannsee" refers to the meeting held in Berlin on January 20, 1942. Otmar Freyherr von Verschuer's disciple

and collaborator was Dr. Josef Mengele. (See Robert Jay Lifton, *The Nazi Doctors*, New York: Basic Books, 1986.) The list of names refers to those indicted at the Nuremberg trials who were never convicted, or simply disappeared.

57   The poem originally appeared with the title "A zsidó menyasszony" (The Jewish Bride), and was dedicated to Gábor Schein. Compare with Gábor Schein's poem ("városnézes hármasban") [three gazes onto the city] (in: *Üveghal*, Budapest: Magvető, 2001, p. 18).

For their comments and encouragement, thanks are owed to—among many others—Nikolai Bojkov, Attila Jász, Tibor Keresztury, Sándor Mészáros, Tamás József Rémenyi, and Márton Lajos Varga.

Translator's Afterword

FIRST PUBLISHED in Hungarian in 2003, *Berlin-Hamlet* was the sixth volume of poetry by Szilárd Borbély (1963–2014). Borbély, who lectured at the University of Debrecen, was a specialist in late-Baroque Central European literature, as well as a highly regarded dramatist, and the author of the widely praised novel *The Dispossessed* (2013). For the Hungarian literary world, he was universally viewed, even across lines of aesthetic or political disagreement, as one of the leading figures in the first generation of authors to emerge following the end of Communism. His tragic death by suicide at the age of fifty meant the loss of an utterly unique voice for European literature as a whole.

The circumstances of Borbély's life, and particularly the broad social impact of the semiautobiographical *The Dispossessed*—which, as it happened, was the last work published in his lifetime—could well overshadow his actual written legacy. Without in any way lessening the importance of his prose, his criticism, or his verse-dramas, it is necessary to stress that he was predominantly a poet, and a poet working within the vital poetic community of generational cohorts that existed in the first decade of the new millennium. Moreover, his oeuvre displays an incredible range of variation in styles and themes. The successor volume to *Berlin-Hamlet*, entitled *Halotti pompa: Szekvenciák* (Final Matters: Sequences, 2004), does contain poems that bear similarities to Borbély's previous work, yet only as a single section out of three radically diverging yet equally positioned treatments of the subject of death. This "modern" component expresses, in startling paradox, the pagan, Greco-Roman view of human mortality, yet it is situated as the interstice between two deliberate appropriations of far older forms at the very margins of Hungarian literature: the Catholic devotional folk poetry of the eighteenth century and the parables of the Hungarian-speaking Szatmár Hasidic rabbinical mystics of Hungary's rural northwest. And the volume that followed, *A Testhez* (*To the Body*, 2010), presented yet another shift: philosophical abstractions that push the meaningful possibilities of Hungarian to the ultimate end of expression alternate with scourging raw testimonies in a variety of narrative voices.

Nonetheless, the common strands linking all of Borbély's publications lie in their exceptional consistency of ethical and artistic vision. All clichés of the Central European poet as "national conscience" or "unelected legislator" aside, Borbély for all his life held strongly to the vision of poetry as a moral act. A sizable tendency of post-1989 Hungarian literature was for stylistic experiment (or conversely, a return to traditional verse as its own display of postmodernist technical virtuosity) to take precedence over claims towards the exercising of moral authority. Understandably, this development was a natural reaction to both the end of external political pressures as well as the passing of the generation of Hungarian poets (Ágnes Nemes Nagy, Sándor Weöres, János Pilinszky) who survived war and persecution to create exceptional works of verbal art under the complex circumstances of János Kádár's "soft dictatorship" from the mid-1960s onwards. Borbély's lifelong oeuvre, by contrast, represents his own attempt to bring the weight of ethical responsibility into a world of new conditions and challenges. Yet it is less of a reassumption of the stance of the poet as ethical arbiter than a shift to the position of the poet as witness: as a Hungarian writer whose own extended family was not spared the brutalities of World War II, as well as a European thinker closely attuned to his continent's horrors in the past century.

To read *Berlin-Hamlet* is an experience akin to strolling through one of the phantasmagoric shopping arcades described in Walter Benjamin's *Arcades Project*—but instead of window displays boasting the remnants of nineteenth-century European optimism, we pass by disembodied scraps of written text from the far ghostlier realm of early twentieth-century modernity: primarily Franz Kafka, yet also including Benjamin himself, or such canonical Hungarian authors as Attila József or Ernő Szép. Structurally, the individual free-verse poems are grouped into five interwoven cycles, with each poem indicated by number.

The cycle "Letter" is based directly upon a series of

quotations taken from the Hungarian translation of the diaries and letters of Franz Kafka. Whether addressed to Kafka's fiancée Felice Bauer (most frequently), Max Brod, Grete Bloch, or simply the diary page, these extracted citations are quite frequently subjected to a visible process of rewriting. Unexpected gaps are inserted, or divergent fragments are placed next to each other in a process of textual montage; in other instances, where Kafka's own letters remain only as fragments, Borbély completes the text himself. Empirically, of course, Kafka did have a personal link with Berlin in his visits to the city to see Felice. In another sense, though, the very presence of Kafka himself in a volume so closely plotted onto the topography of Berlin is a kind of "quotation," extracting the author from his oft-invoked associations with Prague to paste him—shorn of the accretions of myth and stereotype—in a framework that stresses his "Hamlet-like" indecisiveness and ambivalence.

In the second series of poems, each one bears the name of a specific Berlin location or district, immediately describing Borbély's sojourn in that city during the mid-1990s. These poems evoke, with startling concreteness, what time has made of yet another lost era: "unification-era" Berlin, haunted equally by its tragic past as by its present frenzy to rebuild. From the evocatively romantic undergrowth of the Tiergarten to the flickering television sets in the windows of concrete high-rise housing blocks in the grim eastern suburbs, from the cranes above Potsdamer Platz to the homeless beggars and migrant construction workers at the refreshment stands: these descriptions hardly match the then-prevalent triumphal narratives of Europe's unification and history's end. Like Benjamin's emblematic figure of the flaneur for nineteenth-century Paris, the poet wanders fluidly through the actual city, as well as through the mental landscape that he brings to the urban topography—a radically non-hierarchical assemblage with room for U2 videos and Peter Greenaway films alongside classical myths and personal memories or preoccupations. "We know that, in the course of flanerie, far-off times and places interpenetrate the landscape and the present moment"—so Benjamin observed in his *Arcades Project*, noting "the authentically intoxicated phase of this condition." And it is no accident that Benjamin himself is present, through quotation of his memoir *A Berlin Childhood* in the poem "Magdeburger Platz" and, in a more spectral form, in the "Tiergarten" sequences.

The series of verses entitled "Epilogue," positioned only near the very beginning and at the end of the volume, are devoid of concrete historical references of any sort, yet they seem to have been written in the aftermath of calamity; they are, in essence, meditations on the task of the survivor and of rendering tragedy into art. "The recounting of the drawn-out / scream exacts renunciation" ("Epilogue I"), whereas the final cycle is truly remarkable for its evocation of a nearly Talmudic vision of tragedy's culmination.

And finally, an even greater level of abstraction, even to the extent of evading all attempts at definition, is visible in the sequences under the titles "Allegory" and "Fragment." The "Fragment" poems all take as their starting point the dilemma of dialogue with an unspecified inter-locutor, embracing problematics of dissimulation, mimicry, authenticity, resolve: "As if an actor were performing in my stead / I twist the words within myself like a dagger—my wish," the most "Shakespearian" of *Berlin-Hamlet*'s figures states while at the same time evoking the last words of Kafka's *The Trial*. In turn, the "Allegory" poems emerge as allegorical readings of the most quotidian contemporary settings, transforming themselves into a nearly ritualistic search for meaning. Yet however abstract the philosophical language may appear, even in these poems the horror of the past is not far away:

> And I thought of my relatives,
> the ones whom I could never meet. Who
> hovered for a while above the German-Polish
>   lowlands, as
> dust and ashes.

All the more terrifying, the calamity itself is only rarely mentioned explicitly (with the exception of only two poems: "Wannsee" and "Stephansdom"). We are constantly in the company of either those who came before (Kafka, Benjamin) or after (that is, the poet himself in a Germany long subjected to the process of *Vergangenheitsbewältigung*).

Shakespeare's Hamlet, with his fatal inability to act, long served as a totem-figure for the intellectuals of Central Europe in the years between the inferno of World War II and the dissolution of Communist rule. The most widely cited variant of the "Hamlet of Mitteleuropa" was put forward in the writings of Czesław Miłosz and repeatedly cited within Polish literature and essayistic discussion: Hamlet's introspective soul-searching versus the temptations of taking action on the side of power. Miłosz, of course, validated Hamlet's reflectiveness over the victorious survival of Fortinbras; one illustration of the opposing stance is a satirical sketch by the talented poet Konstanty Ildefons Gałczyński (written on the verge of his own submission to the dictates of Stalinist cultural policy): Hamlet enters a café, and unable to choose between coffee or tea, "immediately dies of indecision."

Nonetheless, Miłosz's agonistic moral schema offers only a very imprecise key for deciphering the trope of Hamlet in Hungarian writing, or for that matter, for understanding Hungarian writing in general. Crucial in this regard is a volume of poetry dating from 1968, *Töredék Hamletnek* (A Fragment for Hamlet) by Dezső Tandori—incidentally one of the translators to work on the Hungarian edition of Kafka's diaries and letters used by Borbély in the present volume. Tandori's "fragments"—terse, strongly anti-lyrical, frequently balanced on the edge between sense and unintelligibility—are now considered a major turning point for the Hungarian poetic imagination. The deliberate embrace of a "ruined language" (*rontott nyelv*), which Hungarian critics have discerned in many authors of the late twentieth century, was not necessarily a protest against the malevolent effects of totalitarian ideology on human language (though of course it can and does include this phenomenon in its scope). Rather, as the critic László Bedecs has noted, Tandori's choice of programmatic incompleteness is more often viewed as a philosophical response to the crisis of both language and ideology in the second half of the twentieth century, to the inability to escape from rigid Aristotelian logic and embrace paradox in full.

In contrast to Tandori, who looked to Zen Buddhism for inspiration, *Berlin-Hamlet* remains firmly positioned in the single mental locality of a Germanic Central Europe. Yet the poetics of the incomplete are no less strong for all that. In Bedecs's formulation, the language-ruins of Hungarian poetry of the late twentieth century should not be confused with Europe's long-standing Romantic fetish of the ruin as synecdoche, of the evocation of a bygone whole. Rather, the fragments make fully clear the impossibility of resurrecting, or even conceiving, any form of wholeness: "the fundamental element of fragmentation is absence."

Fragments are inherently ambiguous, and it is the tolerance of unresolved ambiguity that finally brings together the various metaphor Hamlets: Miłosz's detached intellectual, Tandori's first Western adept of Zen, and the several Berlin-Hamlets of the present volume (Kafka, Benjamin, the unnamed narrative voice...) Indeed, the multifocality of these last figures underscores Borbély's deeply ambiguous stance towards the very linguistic medium of his poetry. Hamlet's garbled speech and mystifying paradoxes offer him protection from his pursuers; the unnamed narrator proclaims that he "can no longer bear the aggressiveness of poetry" and places himself in the position of both executioner and victim. Wielding poetic language corresponds equally to the murderer and the murdered; between Henri-ette Vogel's death on the banks of the Wannsee, shot in her suicide pact with the great Romantic dramatist Heinrich von Kleist, and the millions of deaths arranged in a subur-ban villa beside the same lake just over a century later lies only the most ambivalent of lines.

In response, *Berlin-Hamlet* places especial stress on two closely interrelated tactics of composition: the copy and the quotation. Both are, after all, a method of fragmentation, the copy removing the original from its immediate network of connotations and associations, the quotation even more radically stressing the absence of the surrounding linguistic "tissue." The postmodern aesthetic that arose in the West-ern world during the final years of the Cold War placed great stress on an aesthetic of reproduction, from Borges's tale of Pierre Menard and his replication of two chapters from *Don Quixote* through Sherrie Levine's re-creation of iconic pho-tographs. Yet despite the obvious similarities, even despite the shared intellectual background (Benjamin's reflection on mechanical reproduction, the modernism of Weimar Germany), *Berlin-Hamlet* is definitively the product of a radically different attitude towards the process of artistic reproduction, of radically different historical circum-stances. Nothing could be farther from this volume than the would-be "revolutionary" gestures of casting doubt on creative originality. "Allegory V" opens with a thoroughly mundane image, one familiar to all museumgoers: amateur painters "like hunters or fishermen" at work on their cop-ies of well-known old masters. At the heart of the scene, though, is the evocation of a deep-lying horror: the painting being copied depicts a Jewish wedding ceremony (explained only in an authorial footnote), terrifying not for its actual subject but for the retroactive knowledge that we, the viewers of the post-Holocaust age, necessarily impose upon it.

Copying the painting, an action repeated "seven times in one life" by the unnamed figures at their easels, is itself an enactment of the horror, a repetition of the inexpressible catastrophe within the purportedly innocent existence of the artwork. As with the visual copy, the literary quotation, whether an exact reproduction or a paraphrase, has its own association in the Western world with certain strategies of postmodern writing, in particular the practice of a "paraliterature" that itself questions the authorial voice and authorial creation. Unquestionably, Hungarian literature since the onset of postmodernity has taken up the quotation-palimpsest with great fervor. There is hardly any significant Hungarian writer of the present who altogether refrains from explicit quotation; perhaps one of the most extreme instances is Péter Esterházy's *Helping Verbs of the Heart*, in which quotations from an incredible variety of sources are woven seamlessly into the text. At the same time, the Hungarian practice of quotation and re-quotation differs from the version set forth by poststructuralist theoreticians, even on the level of the term used for it: *vendégszöveg*, literally "guest" or "substitute text." Rather than striking a pose of radical questioning, it draws upon the presumption of its readers' intimate knowledge of a specific group of canonical Hungarian literary works, primarily those of the first half of the twentieth century. Alongside the "guest-texts" originating in the German-speaking world, *Berlin-Hamlet* also invokes another lost realm: that of Hungary before the scourges of Hitler and Stalin and their Hungarian collaborators. In particular, the ghostly presences behind several of the poems are Attila József (1905–1937), the brilliant poet dead by his own hand on the very eve of the cataclysm of World War II, and Ernő Szép (1884–1953), a poet of Jewish origin consigned to slave labor under Fascist rule, who survived yet allegedly introduced himself, throughout the postwar years, in the past tense. Elucidation of all of the periphrastic wisps of József or Szép to be found in *Berlin-Hamlet* would, of course, take far more space than allotted to a typical afterword. Nor, more important, is the exact knowledge of the specifically Hungarian references necessary for an understanding of the individual poems: the "guest-texts" are in no way inserted as a hidden code to be deciphered but simply form yet another of the multiple layers of textuality.

Rettet die Ruinen—rescue the ruins—ran a widespread shibboleth of Berlin's counterculture during the 1990s. *Berlin-Hamlet* makes no such strident appeal, nor does it offer any vain illusion of rescue or resuscitation for the destroyed Mitteleuropa of Kafka, Benjamin, or Szép. Yet through the fragments, and through the knowledge of what agency brought about the shattering, this volume does lead us into that vanished world.

—*Ottilie Mulzet*

DANTE ALIGHIERI THE NEW LIFE
Translated by Dante Gabriel Rossetti; Preface by Michael Palmer

KINGSLEY AMIS COLLECTED POEMS: 1944–1979

GUILLAUME APOLLINAIRE ZONE: SELECTED POEMS
Translated by Ron Padgett

SZILÁRD BORBÉLY BERLIN-HAMLET
Translated by Ottilie Mulzet

NAJWAN DARWISH NOTHING MORE TO LOSE
Translated by Kareem James Abu-Zeid

BENJAMIN FONDANE CINEPOEMS AND OTHERS
Edited by Leonard Schwartz

SAKUTARŌ HAGIWARA CAT TOWN
Translated by Hiroaki Sato

MIGUEL HERNÁNDEZ *Selected and translated by Don Share*

LOUISE LABÉ LOVE SONNETS AND ELEGIES
Translated by Richard Sieburth

OSIP MANDELSTAM VORONEZH NOTEBOOKS
Translated by Andrew Davis

SILVINA OCAMPO *Selected and translated by Jason Weiss*

J.H. PRYNNE THE WHITE STONES *Introduction by Peter Gizzi*

A. K. RAMANUJAN THE INTERIOR LANDSCAPE: CLASSICAL
TAMIL LOVE POEMS

PIERRE REVERDY *Edited by Mary Ann Caws*

ALEXANDER VVEDENSKY AN INVITATION FOR ME TO THINK
Translated by Eugene Ostashevsky and Matvei Yankelevich

WALT WHITMAN DRUM-TAPS: THE COMPLETE 1865 EDITION
Edited by Lawrence Kramer

ELIZABETH WILLIS ALIVE: NEW AND SELECTED POEMS